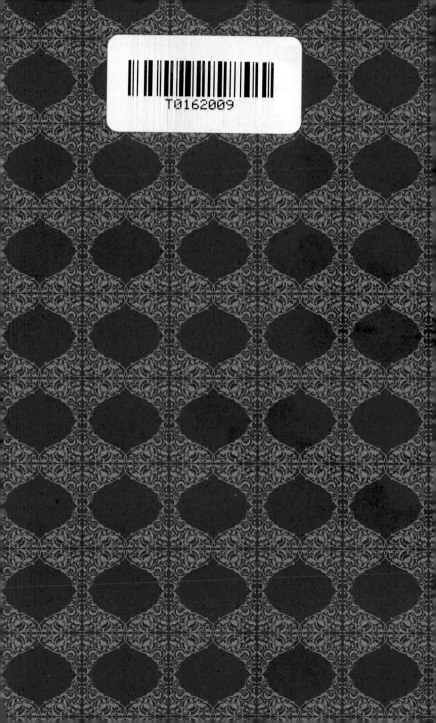
T0162009

BLESSED NAMES AND ATTRIBUTES
of
Allah ﷻ

Abdur Raheem Kidwai

KUBE
PUBLISHING

Blessed Names and Attributes of Allah ﷻ

First published in England by

Kube Publishing Ltd
Markfield Conference Centre
Ratby Lane, Markfield,
Leicestershire LE67 9SY
United Kingdom
Tel: +44 (0) 1530 249230
Fax: +44 (0) 1530 249656
Website: www.kubepublishing.com
Email: info@kubepublishing.com

© Abdur Raheem Kidwai, 2016
All rights reserved.
7[th]impression 2024

The right of Abdur Raheem Kidwai to be
identified as the author of this work has been
asserted by him in accordance with the
Copyright, Designs and Patents Act, 1988.

Cataloguing-in-Publication Data
is available from the British Library

ISBN 978 1 84774 087 8 *casebound*

Typeset N.A. Qaddoura
Design Imtiaze Ahmed
Printed in Turkey by Elma Basim

CONTENTS

TRANSLITERATION TABLE

Arabic Consonants

Initial, unexpressed medial and final: ء ʾ

ا	a	د	d	ض	ḍ	ك	k
ب	b	ذ	dh	ط	ṭ	ل	l
ت	t	ر	r	ظ	ẓ	م	m
ث	th	ز	z	ع	ʿ	ن	n
ج	j	س	s	غ	gh	هـ	h
ح	ḥ	ش	sh	ف	f	و	w
خ	kh	ص	ṣ	ق	q	ي	y

With a *shaddah*, both medial and final consonants are doubled.

Vowels, diphthongs, etc.

Short:	َ a	ِ i	ُ u
Long:	َا ā	ِي ī	ُو ū
Diphthongs:		َوْ aw	
		َيْ ay	

PREFACE

THIS work represents a compendium, listing and elu-
cidating 99 excellent names of Allah which figure in
the Qur'ān and standard Ḥadīth collections. Both the
Qur'ān and Aḥādīth (plural) state the importance of
learning these beautiful names, and promise reward
for those who invoke Allah in their supplications with
reference to His excellent names. These names offer
a conspectus of the articles of Islamic faith and intro-
duce concisely the being and attributes of Allah.

With its elucidation of an important facet of Islamic
faith, the present work supplements and complements
the earlier three volumes of the series *Daily Wisdom*,
brought out by Kube Publishing, which explicate
select Qur'ānic passages, Aḥādīth, and Islamic prayers
and supplications, respectively. It is hoped this volume
too, will enable readers to gain a better understanding
of Islamic faith. Written in simple, easy to understand
English, the present work seeks to bring out the lesson
conveyed to us by each name of Allah. Its study may
enable readers to appreciate better the Islamic scheme

of things about this world and the next and instruct us how to invoke Allah in our supplications and petitions to Him. This work may facilitate, also, our conceptualization of Allah Whose glory and greatness is limitless.

I must thank Brothers Yahya Birt and Haris Ahmad of Kube Publishing, UK for having entrusted this valuable assignment to me, notwithstanding my inadequacies. May Allah accept this modest effort (Āmīn).

Abdur Raheem Kidwai
Professor, Department of English
Aligarh Muslim University, India
Muḥarram 1437 AH
October 2015 CE

بسم الله الرحمن الرحيم

INTRODUCTION

Allah's are the names most beautiful. Whatever is in the heavens and the earth extols His glory.

(al-Ḥashr 59: 24)

Allah – there is no God but He. His are the most excellent names.

(Ṭā Hā 20: 8)

Say to them (O Prophet!): "Call upon Him as Allah or call upon Him as Al-Raḥmān; call Him by which-ever name you will, all His names are beautiful".

(al-Isrā' 17: 110)

Allah has the most excellent names. So call on Him by His names and shun those who distort them.

(al-A'rāf 7: 180)

Apart from the above Qur'ānic assertions, the ex-cellence of Allah's name is also pressed home by the following Aḥādīth:

On the authority of Abū Hurayrah, it is related that the Prophet (peace be upon him) said: "Allah has 99 names. Whoever remembers these, will enter Paradise." Companions report that they had memorized and counted these names well.

(Bukhārī, *Kitāb Al-Tawḥīd*, 2, 1,099)

Another report recounted by Abū Hurayrah is as follows: "Allah has 99 names. He who remembers these will certainly enter Paradise."

(Bukhārī, *Kitāb Al-Daʿawāt*, 2, 949)

Abū Hurayrah quotes the Prophet (peace be upon him) saying: "Allah 99 names. He who memorizes these is destined to enter Paradise".

(Muslim, *Kitāb Al-Dhikr wa Al-Duʿāʾ*, 2, 342)

According to Tirmidhī, Abū Hurayrah reports that the Prophet (peace be upon him) said: "Allah has 99 names. He who learns these by heart will enter Paradise". Tirmidhī adds that this Ḥadīth does not specify those 99 names of Allah and that it is a *ḥasan ṣaḥīḥ* Ḥadīth.

(Tirmidhī, *Abwāb Al-Daʿawāt*, 2, 188–9)

In his gloss over *Jāmi' Al-Tirmidhī,* Qāḍī Abū Bakr ibn 'Arabī maintains that there are 1,000 names of Allah and the Prophet Muḥammad (peace be upon him) each.

(Maqrīzī, *Imtā' Al-Asmā',* 2, 138)

These divine names provide a graphic account of Allah's attributes. While going through these, we realize how perfect and unique He is. His excellent names evoke our love, fear and admiration for Him. We should gain a clear understanding of His names, memorize these and act in accordance with the message imparted by these. As noted in Aḥādīth, this will *inshā' Allāh* facilitate our entry into Paradise. If we assimilate their message, we will enjoy a peaceful, happy life in this world both as individuals and as a community.

The Qur'ān brands these as "excellent" names in view of these considerations: (i) Since Allah is Perfect, Unique and the Most Exalted, His names underscore the same. It is common knowledge that a being is known and characterized by the name. (ii) As we memorize and grasp the meaning of these names, we are in a better position to bring to our mind His greatness and glory when we invoke Him, especially for seeking His help and favours. In that state our whole being testifies to His numerous and perfect attributes. (iii) There is no one equal unto Allah in His glorious and excellent attributes. Since He has spelled out His names, our invocation to Him by these names may prompt His mercy and pleasure.

We are told in Ḥadīth reports that Allah's love for His creatures exceeds far more than mother's love for her child. As we address Him by His authentic names, we are more likely to get some response to our petitions to Him.

Invoking Allah with reference to these names and memorizing these amounts to this Qur'ānic mode of worship of glorifying and mentioning Allah:

Believers Remember Allah much and glorify Him morning and evening.

(al-Aḥzāb 33: 41–42)

It goes without saying that this exercise of mentioning Allah's name inspirits us. The Qur'ān affirms the same:

Believers are those who believe (in Allah and the message of the Prophet) and whose hearts find rest in the remembrance of Allah. Surely in Allah's remembrance do hearts find rest.

(al-Raʿd 13: 28)

Moreover, the use of His names in our supplications enables us to focus on His perfect being and excellent attributes. This, in turn, renders our prayers more fervent and earnest. Studying and memorizing the excellent names of Allah is, thus, an act of devotional worship for which Allah has promised to reward us. Moreover, this study of Allah's names and attributes provides us with an opportunity to gain or renew our acquaintance with the Islamic worldview as a whole.

Reading about his names presents before us a vivid, comprehensive picture of the articles of Islamic faith. More importantly, this study helps us draw upon Allah's boundless mercy and affection. It inculcates into us love, respect and regard for Allah. On reading these names and attributes we are drawn closer to our Lord and Creator, Allah and appreciate better the meaning and message of the Prophet's noble mission.

In view these considerations, the Qur'ān makes some pointed references to Allah's names. The Companions regarded it as their great privilege to record, elucidate and transmit the *Aḥādīth* on the excellent names of Allah and attributes.

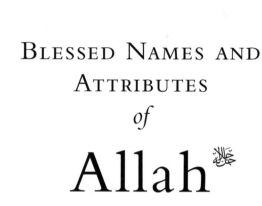

Blessed Names and Attributes

of

Allah ﷻ

I

ALLAH / GOD

THIS name is unique to God in the Islamic parlance. The Qur'ānic Sūrah al–Ikhlāṣ provides this helpful account of Him: "*He is Allah, the Eternal, Ever-Living. He neither begot any nor was He begotten. And none is comparable to Him.*" (al-Ikhlāṣ 112: 1-4) He is the Creator and Sustainer of the entire universe.

From Sūrah al-Fātiḥah 1: 1

2

THE MOST MERCIFUL

IT is one of the recurrent names of Allah in the Qur'ān. For mercy is a dominant attribute of Allah. We possess all that we have owing to His mercy. While keeping in mind this excellent name of Allah we should be kind and helpful to fellow human beings. Likewise, we should make it a point to follow the way prescribed by Him, Who is Most Merciful. It is in our own interest to do only that to which the Most Merciful One has guided us. The following Prophetic supplication brings out the centrality of this divine name:

اللَّهُمَّ فَارِجَ الْهَمِّ كَاشِفَ الْغَمِّ مُجِيبَ دَعْوَةِ الْمُضْطَرِّيْنَ رَحْمَـٰنَ الدُّنْيَا وَالْآخِرَةِ وَرَحِيْمَهُمَا أَنْتَ تَرْحَمُنِيْ فَارْحَمْنِيْ بِرَحْمَةٍ تُغْنِيْنِيْ بِهَا عَنْ رَحْمَةٍ مَنْ سِوَاكَ

(الحاكم، ج-١ ، ص ٥١٥)

❧ 4 ❧

O Lord! Reliever of worry, Remover of anxiety, Responder to the call of those under duress, the Merciful and the Mercy-Giver in this world and in the Hereafter. It is You Who will have mercy on me in a way that frees me from seeking mercy from anyone besides You.

(al-Ḥākim)

3

THE MOST COMPASSIONATE

------ ·•· ------

LIKE *Al-Raḥmān*, this divine name *Al-Raḥīm* often appears in the Qur'ān. Allah's compassion towards us consists in:

- His overlooking our sins and accepting our repentance;
- His blessing us with numerous bounties;
- His affection for us in both this world and the next;
- His granting rewards to us in Paradise;
- His favours to us, without asking for anything in return which may benefit Him.

From Sūrah al-Fātiḥah 1: 1

4

THE TRUE KING

———— ·•· ————

ALLAH alone is the true King and we, being His
subjects, are obliged to abide by His commands. This
alone may prove our loyalty to Him. There have been
kings in the world. But it is common knowledge that
even great kings rule for a brief period of time and
over a small part of the world. Allah's Kingship is total
and encompasses all that is in the universe.

Ṭā Hā 20: 114

From Sūrah

5

THE HOLY

THE divine name brings out Allah's perfection as He is free from any blemish. Being the servants of the Holiest One, we should try our best to cleanse ourselves by doing good, and keeping away from sin and evil. This may help us attain righteousness to a degree. The Prophet Muḥammad's fondness for this divine name is reflected in this prayer formula which he used to recite after *witr* (odd numbered) Prayer:

سُبْحَانَ الْمَلِكِ الْقُدُّوسِ، سُبْحَانَ الْمَلِكِ الْقُدُّوسِ، سُبْحَانَ الْمَلِكِ القُدُّوسِ ، سُبُّوحٌ قُدُّوسٌ، رَبُّ الْمَلَائِكَةِ وَالرُّوحُ

(مسلم، كتاب الصّلاة، ص ٢٢٣)

Glory be to the King, the Holy! Glory be to the King, the Holy! Glory be to the King, the Holy! Blessed be the Holy One, the Lord of angels and the spirit.

(Muslim, *Kitāb al-Salāh*)

From Sūrah al-Ḥashir 59: 23

﹌ 8 ﹌

6

السَّلَامُ

THE ALL PEACE

Allah is the source of all peace and security. Moreover, He loves peace and order. This is evident from the Islamic norm of salutation: "*Assalāmu 'Alaykum*" (peace be on you). The Prophet Muḥammad's devotion to this divine name figures in this supplication which he used to recite at the conclusion of every Prayer:

اللَّهُمَّ أَنْتَ السَّلَامُ وَمِنْكَ السَّلَامُ تَبَارَكْتَ يَا ذَا الْجَلَالِ وَالْإِكْرَامْ

(أبو داود، باب الدعاء، ص٢٦٠)

O Lord! You are All Peace and all peace is only from You. Blessed be You, full of majesty and splendour.
(Abū Dāwūd, *Bāb al-Du'ā'*)

From Sūrah al-Ḥashr 59: 23

7

THE ONE WHO GIVES SECURITY

From Sūrah al-Ḥashr 59: 23

By bestowing faith upon us and by showing the way leading to Him, Allah provides our souls with security and inner peace. This saves us from stumbling into the darkness of superstition, disbelief and unbelief. As thanksgiving for this immense favour we should strengthen our faith which will accrue to us peace and security. Moreover, we should lead life in a way which is characterized by peace and tranquility. The remembrance of His excellent name is in our own interest, in that it keeps our inner being and our social fabric intact and safe against disorder and chaos.

8

THE OVERSEER

IT goes without saying that we exist and survive because of Allah's care and protection. Again, it is He Who has granted us safety and security. Being the perfect Overseer, He will recompense everyone in the Afterlife with complete justice.

From Sūrah al-Hashr 59: 23

9

THE MOST MIGHTY

NOT only is Allah Most Mighty, He also exercises His unchallenged power with utmost kindness, justice and forgiveness. Those of us whom Allah has blessed with some authority should strive to imbue the above traits. Moreover, since Allah alone enjoys all power and might, we must turn only to Him for all help. Only He can rescue man and meet all of his needs, in that He enjoys absolute power and can execute all that He wills.

10

THE OVERPOWERING

ALLAH, the Overpowering One, salvages us in our crisis and comforts and consoles us in our loss and sorrow. Moreover, it is He Who enables us to see and follow the straight way which will accrue success to us in this world and the next. In recognition of the truth embodied in this divine name, the Prophet (peace be upon him) recited this supplication:

سُبْحَانَ ذِيْ الْمُلْكِ وَالْمَلَكُوْتِ وَالْجَبَرُوْتِ
وَالْكِبْرِيَاءِ وَالْعَظَمَةِ

(الطبراني، المعجم، ج-١٠، ص١٢)

Glory be to Allah Who owns all kingdom, dominion, glory, greatness and splendour.

(Al-Ṭabarānī, *al-Muʿjam*)

From Sūrah al-Ḥashr *59: 23*

11

ALL GREAT

ALLAH is All Great, for He excels over all and transcends everything. In view of His greatness, which is manifest around us, we must surrender ourselves wholly to Him and lead our lives marked by modesty and humility. We should realize our total subservience to Him and treat all of His creatures with love and affection.

12

THE CREATOR

This self evident truth should be clearly imbibed by us; that Allah has created all that exists, including the heavens and the earth and what is between these. Moreover, He is the Creator without equal. For each creature of His is unique and delightful. His countless creative wonders are reflective of His creativity and greatness.

From Sūrah al-Anʿām 6: 117

13

البَارِئُ

THE CREATOR

From Sūrah   al-Ḥashr 59: 24

WHILE it is common knowledge that Allah is the Creator, His name *al-Bārī* signifies, in particular, His creative power; of bringing things out of nothing, of designing things without any pre-existing model and of creating whatever He wills in a fashion of His choice. Of course, no one shares with Him this amazing creative faculty.

The Prophet Moses (peace be upon him) advised his community members: "*Turn in repentance to your Creator.*" (al-Baqarah 2: 54) We should always remain conscious of our servitude to our Creator Who brought us into being out of nothing and to Whom we owe everything.

14

المُصَوِّرُ

THE FASHIONER OF CREATION

———•———

ALLAH brings everything and everyone into being out of nothing. He provides living souls to lifeless bodies. More remarkably, there is inexhaustible variety in His creation. Take any natural object of the physical world as an illustration. Its various and unique features are bewildering. The same holds true for the plant and animal species which represent astounding variety and colour. Being the perfect Fashioner, Allah accomplishes all this.

From Sūrah al-Ḥashir 59: 24

15

الْغَفَّارُ

THE MOST FORGIVING

OUT of His tremendous mercy Allah keeps overlooking and forgiving our sins. As our deliverance in the Afterlife is contingent upon His forgiveness, we must keep seeking His forgiveness. We should follow, in this respect, the Prophet's example, who invoked Allah's forgiveness thus:

اللَّهُمَّ أَنْتَ رَبِّي لَا اِلٰهَ الاَّ أَنْتَ خَلَقْتَنِي وَأَنَا عَبْدُكَ وَأَنَا عَلَى
عَهْدِكَ وَوَعْدِكَ مَا اسْتَطَعْتُ أَعُوذُ بِكَ مِنْ شَرِّ مَا صَنَعْتُ أَبُوْءُ
لَكَ بِنِعْمَتِكَ عَلَيَّ وَأَبُوْءُ بِذَنْبِي فَاغْفِرْلِي إِنَّهُ لاَ يَغْفِرُ الذُّنُوْبَ الاَّ أَنْتَ

(البخاري، كتاب الدعوات، ص ١٤٣)

O Allah! You are my Lord. There is no god besides You. I am Your slave and You have created me. I will hold true to Your promise and pledge as much as is in my power. I seek refuge in You from the evil You

have created. I acknowledge Your blessings showered on me and I admit my sins. So, forgive me. For none forgives sins except You.

(Bukhārī, *Kitāb al-Daʿawāt*)

16

THE IRRESISTIBLE

ALLAH'S total control over us and over all that is around us should make us all the more submissive and obedient to, and fearful of, Him. His mastery over the heavens and the earth and what is between these is an undeniable reality.

17

الوَهَّابُ

THE MUNIFICENT GIVER

ALLAH gives us His bounties consistently, and without asking for anything in return. The Qur'ān cites some of His munificent bounties, as for example the two sons, the Prophets Ishmael and Isaac (peace be upon them) to the Prophet Abraham (peace be upon him) in his old age. As *Al-Wahhāb* He showered His choicest blessings upon His Messengers. This represents His boundless mercy. On reflection, it dawns upon us that we do not actually possess anything; everything with us is the favour of the Munificent Giver.

From Sūrah Āl ʿImrān 3: 8

18

الرَّزَّاقُ

THE BESTOWER OF ALL PROVISIONS

From Sūrah al-Dhāriyāt 51: 58

ALLAH is the Bestower of all provisions on an unfath-omable scale. All animate beings and inanimate things are sustained by Him, all the time. The variety and quantum of His provisions is equally breath-taking. Furthermore, as the Sustainer of everyone, He grants provisions to all, including even those who do not believe, rather mock Him. Such magnanimity and perfect justice is unthinkable for any human being, no matter how generous he might be. While recall-ing Allah's numerous provisions to us, we should help those in need and share with them what Allah has bestowed more lavishly on us.

19

الْفَتَّاحُ

THE GREAT JUDGE

As Allah is All Powerful and All Knowing, He alone
does and can perform as the Great Judge. Moreover,
in the same capacity He lets man distinguish between
truth and falsehood.

With reference to this divine name the Prophet
Muḥammad (peace be upon him) has taught us this
comprehensive supplication:

اللهُمَّ إِنِّي أَسْئَلُكَ فَوَاتِحَ الْخَيْرِ وَ خَوَاتِمَهُ وَ جَوَامِعَهُ وَ أَوَّلَهُ وأَخِرَهُ

وَظَاهِرَهُ وَبَاطِنَهُ وَالدَّرَجَاتِ الْعُلَى مِنَ الْجَنَّةِ. آمِينْ

(الحاكم، ج-١، ص ٥٢٠)

O Lord! I seek from You good – its beginning and its
end and in its totality. I seek its opening and final parts
and its outward and innermost forms and a high rank
in Paradise. Āmīn!

(Al-Ḥākim)

20

THE ALL AWARE

THIS divine name underscores Allah's perfect and all-encompassing knowledge. More remarkably, He also knows the unseen, including our secret thoughts and the wrong doing committed by our eyes. As to the range of His knowledge, the Qur'ān informs: "*He knows what penetrates into the earth and what goes forth from it ... Nothing escapes Him, not even the smallest particle in the heavens or the earth ...*" (Saba' 34: 2-3)

He grants knowledge, in varying degrees, to His creatures. For gaining better and beneficial knowledge, we should pray to Him because He is the source and provider of all knowledge.

21

THE ONE WHO RESTRICTS

———— •◦• ————

THE Qur'ān informs that, out of His wisdom, Allah grants provisions to His creatures in a certain measure. Likewise, He has kept secure the functioning of the universe by subjecting all of us to His discipline and order. We do not have any role whatsoever in altering His will.

The strict divine dispensation should make us all the more cognizant of His power and our dependence upon Him. We should try to win His pleasure, in that He controls our destiny as He wills.

From Sūrah al-Baqarah 2: 245

22

الْبَاسِطُ

THE ONE WHO EXPANDS

As the Supreme, All Powerful Being, Allah expands whatever He wills, including sustenance for us. We should keep fervently imploring Him for showering His inexhaustible favours on us. He lavishes His bounties on whoever He pleases out of His wisdom and will.

23

THE ONE WHO DEGRADES

WE learn from the Qur'ān that Allah will turn things upside down on the Last Day. We keep observing instances of His degrading whoever He wills. We should, in particular, keep away from pride. For Allah abases the proud in no time.

From Ibn Mājah ❧ Kitāb al-Duʿāʾ: 3,861

24

الرَّافِعُ

THE ONE WHO ELEVATES

Āl ʿImrān 3: 55

From Sūrah

Being All High and All Powerful, Allah elevates who-ever He wills. It is heartening for us to learn from the Qurʾān: *"Allah will raise to high ranks those of you who believe and are endowed with knowledge."* (al-Mujādalah 58: 11) This divine promise should inspire us all the more to use our faculties and knowledge for winning His pleasure. This will result in our elevation by Him, which is undoubtedly the highest reward imaginable.

25

الْمُعِزُّ

THE ONE WHO EXALTS

HERE is an awe-inspiring Qur'ānic proclamation: *"(O Prophet), say: 'O Allah, Lord of all dominion! You exalt whom You please, and abase whom You please. In Your hand is all good. Surely You are All Powerful.'"* (Āl 'Imrān 3: 26) This phenomenon is all before us, apart from its ample documentation in history. The true honour and exaltation, nonetheless, consist in faith, as the Qur'ān announces: *"In truth, all honour belongs to Allah and to His Messenger, and to the believers."* (al-Munāfiqūn 63: 8)

For reiterating this truth the Prophet (peace be upon him) taught the following supplication to his grandson, Ḥasan:

لَا يَذِلُّ مَنْ وَالَيْتَ وَلَا يَعِزُّ مَنْ عَادَيْتَ

(أبو داود، كتاب الصلوة، ص ٢٤٦)

Indeed, he whom You have taken under Your custody shall not be humiliated. Nor will he against whom You have declared enmity gain any might.

(Abū Dāwūd, *Kitāb al-Ṣalāt*)

26

THE ONE WHO DEGRADES

———— ·•· ————

ALLAH has His own way of exalting and degrading
man. Those exalted by Him are brought low in no
time by Him. We do not have any control or pre-
rogative on this count. We should constantly pray
to Allah for exalting us and for protecting us from
degrading us in both this world and the next. Faith
and devotion to Him are the sure means for attaining
honour and for escaping dishonour.

From Sūrah Āl 'Imrān 3:26

27

THE ALL HEARING

———— ·•· ————

APART from His power and knowledge, this divine name points to Allah's nearness to people and their invocation to Him. Here is an illustration of the range of the All Hearing Allah. This refers to a complaint by the wife of a Companion to the Prophet Muḥammad (peace be upon him) against her husband: "*Allah has surely heard the words of her who contends with you concerning her husband and complains to Allah. Allah hears what both of you say. Allah is All Hearing, All Seeing.*" (al-Mujādalah 58: 1)

Given this, we should sincerely present our cases before Him. He will respond in the manner which is suited best for us.

28

THE ONE WHO SEES

ALLAH sees all, including His servants and their actions, and all that exists in the universe. Interestingly, "*No visual perception can encompass Him, though He encompasses all visual perception.*" (al-Anʿām 6: 103)

Again, it is He Who has blessed us with the faculty of seeing. In view of His all-inclusive sight we should be careful about our actions. For these cannot escape Him.

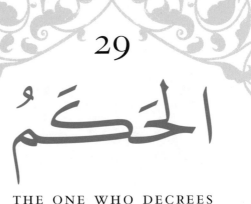

29

الْحَكَمُ

THE ONE WHO DECREES

———— •◆• ————

THE Qur'ān warns us against the ignoble end of the arrogant. In the Afterlife they will roast in the Hell-fire, and say: "*All of us are in it [the Hellfire]. Allah passed His Judgement among His servants.*" (al-Mu'min 40: 48) Since His decree is final and irrevocable, we should obey His commands in order to please Him.

30

THE KNOWER

ALLAH knows all that exists in the heavens and on earth. Moreover, He knows both what is evident and what is hidden. His knowledge of the unseen, which lies totally outside our sense perception, is special to Him.

This divine attribute should make us all the more careful about our answerability to Him.

From Sūrah al-Ḥashr *59: 22*

31

اللَّطِيفُ

THE ALL SUBTLE

From Sūrah al-Anʿām 6: 103

In line with this divine attribute we all benefit from Allah's numerous favours. Needless to add, He has provided us with a variety of material objects which stand out for their beauty, proportion and usefulness. Out of the same divine attribute we are blessed with mental, physical, psychological and spiritual faculties, consciousness, insights, discernment and inclination for doing good.

We therefore owe it to Him that we should act kindly towards everyone and help the needy in particular.

32

THE WELL AWARE

———— ·•· ————

BEING All Knowing, Allah is well aware of all that exists in the heavens and on earth. He knows everything—past, present and future. This should draw us closer to Him, by way of remembering Him constantly, and helping fellow creatures.

From Sūrah al-Baqarah 2:234

33

THE ALL FORBEARING

ALLAH does not punish us instantly for our misdeeds. Nor does He deny His numerous provisions to even those who reject Him and rebel against Him. This constitutes His forbearance. Likewise, His wrath does not overwhelm His mercy or *vice versa*, in that He is perfectly forbearing. He keeps granting a long respite to the sinners so that they may recognize the truth and mend their ways.

What we learn from this divine attribute is a lesson of tolerance, forgiveness and peaceful coexistence. We should put up with any offence and hurt caused to us. Allah is sufficient to take offenders to task.

34

THE ALL GLORIOUS

ALLAH is truly glorious. Take as illustrative His throne
and power, His revelation of the Scriptures, particularly the Qur'ān, His chain of Messengers throughout history for man's guidance, His creation of this
gigantic universe, and His reward and punishment.
The Qur'ān exhorts us to "*glorify the name of the Great
Lord.*" (al-A'lā 87: 1) Accordingly, we recite the same
formula in *rukū'* (bowing down) of each *rak'ah* of
Prayer.

As a tribute to Allah's boundless glory we should
stand before Him in Prayer with utmost humility and
devotion.

35

THE ALL FORGIVING

From Sūrah al-Baqarah 2: 173

THIS divine name appears scores of times in the Qur'ān, pointing to Allah's kindness, love and mercy which He keeps showering upon His servants. We should no doubt have conviction that He may forgive, out of His mercy, our sins. However, we should be very careful about avoiding sins. This divine name should make us steady on the straight path, believing that He will forgive our past misdeeds.

36

THE MOST APPRECIATIVE

NOTWITHSTANDING His not requiring our worship and praise for and obedience to Him, Allah generously appreciates our good actions. By way of His appreciation He enables us to do more good actions.

This divine name and attribute should inspire us to be appreciative of all those who help and support us.

Fāṭir 35: 30

From Sūrah

37

THE MOST EXALTED

THE Qur'ān presents Allah thus: "*The Most Exalted is Allah, the True King!*" (Ṭā Hā 20: 114) In line with the same, we recite "*Subḥāna Rabbī al-A'lā*" (Glory be to the Most Exalted Lord) in prostration, as part of our Prayer. During prostration we place our head on the ground, in acknowledgement of our surrender and humility before the Most Exalted Lord. This may help us gain spiritual elevation.

38

THE ALL GREAT

ALLAH's greatness is self-evident. For all great persons pale into nothing before Him. His greatness is by means of His perfect attributes. However, He is All Great by Himself, and not because of anything. Rather, greatness and honour befit only Him. The Qur'ān asserts it thus: "*His is the glory in the heavens and the earth. He is the Most Mighty, Most Wise.*" (al-Jāthiyah 45: 37)

From Sūrah al-Ḥajj 22: 62

39

THE WATCHFUL ONE

ᵃˡˡᵃ *guards everything and everyone. The entire universe is under His care. Its maintenance does not weary Him at all.* (al–Baqarah 2: 255) He protects us against the accursed Satan and all evil and harm. Out of His vast mercy and affection for His creatures, He guards us. We should repose trust in His protection and entrust all our possessions to His care.

The realization of our constant protection by Allah helps us defeat and fend against evil thoughts prompted by Satan. This in turn enables us to keep following Allah's way and win His pleasure for entering Paradise, which is our ultimate and abiding success.

From Sūrah Saba' 34: 21

40

THE SUSTAINER

BEING All Powerful, Allah sustains everyone and everything, ensuring their growth and flourishing. He sustains us in every respect; physically, spiritually, intellectually and emotionally. We should, therefore, approach only Him for the development and maintenance of all of our faculties. For our health, happiness and well-being on every count we should earnestly pray to Him alone.

From Sūrah al-Nisā' 4: 85

41

THE ONE WHO TAKES ACCOUNT

THE Qur'ān informs us: "*On the Day of Judgement Allah will present before man his record of deeds in the shape of a wide open book, (saying): Read your record; this Day you suffice to take account of yourself.*" (al-Isrā' 17: 14) As the Reckoner, Allah's arrangement is so perfect that on looking at the transparently clear and truthful record of our actions we will realize we are destined for His reward or punishment.

On our reckoning on the Day of Judgement, this report is very instructive: "When someone asked Ibn 'Abbās as to how Allah will call everyone to account at the same time, he replied that as He bestows provision on everyone simultaneously, He will take them to account as well."

We should always bear in mind our accountability to Him and implore Him for His leniency and mercy.

42

الْجَلِيلُ

THE MAGNIFIED ONE WITH POWER

ALLAH's magnificence is evident across the universe. We should bear this in mind all the time and try to gain His pleasure. All glory befits only Him in view of His magnificence.

From Sūrah al-Raḥmān 55: 27

43

الْكَرِيمُ

THE MOST BOUNTIFUL

From Sūrah al-Naml 27: 40

ALLAH is undoubtedly the Most Bountiful, for He sent down the noble Messenger, Prophet Muḥammad (peace be upon him), revealed the noble Qur'ān, promises bounties to the believers and blesses everyone with His numerous favours.

We should thank the Bountiful, Noble Lord as much as possible.

44

THE EVER WATCHFUL

THE Qur'ān proclaims: "*Allah is watchful over everything.*" (al-Aḥzāb 33: 52) Being All Powerful and All Knowing, He watches all that exists. The Prophet Jesus (peace be upon him) is seen acknowledging the same truth in this observation regarding his followers who went astray: "*And when You did recall me, You became the watcher over them.*" (al-Mā'idah 5: 117)

We should be ever conscious of His watching over us. This perception is effective in keeping Satan and base desires at bay.

From Sīrah al-Nisā' 4: 1

45

THE EVER RESPONSIVE

—◆—

ALLAH responds to the call of every supplicant. The Qur'ān directs the Prophet (peace be upon him) to pose this challenging question to the unbelievers: "*Who is it Who heeds the prayers of the distressed when he calls out to Him and Who removes his suffering?*" (al-Naml 27: 62)

Our belief in Allah's nearness and responsiveness should make us all the more obedient and faithful to Him. Moreover, the above divine name should infuse more conviction, sincerity and fervour into our prayers to Allah. We should have the conviction that He will respond to our prayer in the way which suits us best.

46

THE ALL EMBRACING

THE Qur'ān provides readers with this account of
Allah's all-embracing rule and power: "*The east and the
west belong to Allah. To whichever direction you turn, you
will be turning to Allah. Allah is All-Embracing, All-Knowing.*" (al-Baqarah 2: 115) His knowledge, wisdom and
forgiveness are mentioned in particular in the Qur'ān,
complementing His All Embracing Being. In all other
respects too, He is boundless. We should reflect on
this attribute which will in turn persuade us all the
more about His greatness and glory. This will help us
adhere to His guidance more effectively and readily.

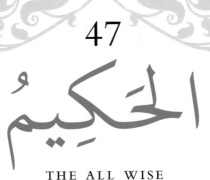

47

الحَكِيمُ

THE ALL WISE

BEING Almighty, All-Aware and All Embracing, Allah
is All-Wise as well. His wisdom is evident from every
manifestation of His creation in terms of its usefulness,
its suitability, its sense of proportion and its excellence.

He granted wisdom to His Messengers and bestows
it on His servants whosoever He wills. The Qur'ān
states: "*Allah grants wisdom to those whom He wills; and
whoever is granted wisdom has been indeed granted much
good.*" (al-Baqarah 2: 269)

Wisdom on our part, in its true sense, consists in
thanking Allah, as is clear from this Qur'ānic directive:
"*Allah bestowed wisdom upon Luqmān, (directing him):
'Give thanks to Allah. Whoso gives thanks to Allah, does so
to his own good.'*" (Luqmān 31: 12) Those of us blessed
with wisdom should also gain the understanding of
faith, pursue knowledge in the broadest sense and
discover and conquer the laws and forces of nature for
the benefit of mankind.

48

الوَدُودُ

THE MOST LOVING

OUT of his immense mercy Allah loves us, as is clear from the Prophet Shu'ayb's directive: "*Seek the forgiveness of your Lord and turn to Him in repentance. Surely my Lord is ever Merciful, Most Loving.*" (Hūd 11: 90) This is the height of our good fortune that Allah has told us that He loves us. His forgiveness, His forbearance and His bestowal of numerous bounties upon us are reflective of His love for us.

Regarding His love for man, the following account recalled by the Prophet (peace be upon him) is quite telling: "While sitting among his Companions the Prophet (peace be upon him) enquired them as to how much a mother loves her child. All of them replied that maternal love is of the highest degree imaginable. Upon this he told them that as compared to Allah's love for His creatures, maternal love is nominal; it represents only a very tiny fraction of the love which Allah has for His creatures."

For reciprocating Allah's abundant love for us, it is binding upon us to worship and serve Him and lead our life obediently in accordance with His way.

49

THE MOST GLORIOUS

ALLAH's being and His exalted Book, the Qur'ān are characterized by utmost glory. The more we reflect upon Allah's favours and creative wonders around us, the better appreciation we will gain about His unmatched glory.

The following Prophetic supplication pays tribute to His glory:

سُبْحَانَ ذِي الْمَجْدِ وَالْكَرَمِ سُبْحَانَ ذِي الْجَلَالِ وَالْإِكْرَامِ

(الطبراني، عن ابن عباس ٤٦٩)

Glory be to Allah Who is Most Glorious, Noblest. Glory be to Allah Who is full of majesty and splendour.

(Al-Ṭabarānī, on the authority of Ibn ʿAbbās)

In recognition of His glory, we should strive hard to win His pleasure which alone can bring about our success in both this life and the Next.

❧ 55 ❧

50

THE SENDER

ALLAH sends down beings, His Messengers and His Scriptures, and His provisions and favours to everyone.

As His servants we are obliged to spread His message among all and to invite people to His way, forbid evil and spread goodness in the world, which will bring about our success in both the worlds.

From Sūrah al-Baqarah 2:213

51

الشَّهِيدُ

THE WITNESS

SINCE Allah is All Knowing, All-Seeing, All-Hearing and All-Powerful, He is understandably the perfect witness as well. For the Qur'ān affirms that "*He is a witness to everything.*" (Saba' 34: 47) Those of us blessed with knowledge should testify to the truth. Our day to day life should also reflect our concern for truth. For example, while acting as a witness, our loyalty should only to be to truth and we should not get swayed by any other consideration. The Prophet (peace be upon him) is on record having branded a false testimony as a major sin:

أَكْبَرُ الْكَبَائِرِ الإِشْرَاكُ بِاللهِ، عُقُوقُ الْوَالِدَيْنِ، شَهَادَةُ الزُّورِ، قَوْلَ الزُّورِ

From Sūrah Āl ʿImrān 3: 98

(البخاري، الأدب، ص ٦)

Major sins are: associating anyone in Allah's divinity, neglecting one's obligations towards parents, giving a false testimony and uttering a false statement.

(Al-Bukhārī, *Kitāb al-Adab*)

52

الْحَقُّ

THE TRUTH

THE truth embodied by Allah is evident in the Qur'ān, faith, and His justice and guidance. For He is the source of truth; calls us to the same, decides everything in truth, sent down His Books and Messengers in truth and has created the universe in truth. He upholds truth and obliterates falsehood. Here is the Prophetic supplication which he used to recite in *tahajjud* (night vigil) prayers, invoking particularly Allah's trait of truth:

وَلَكَ الْحَمْدُ أَنْتَ الْحَقُّ وَوَعْدُكَ حَقٌّ وَالنَّارُ حَقٌّ وَقَوْلُكَ حَقٌّ وَالْجَنَّةُ حَقٌّ وَالنَّارُ حَقٌّ وَالنَّبِيُّونَ حَقٌّ وَمُحَمَّدٌ ﷺ حَقٌّ وَالسَّاعَةُ حَقٌّ

(البخاري، باب التهجد بالليل)

O Allah! All praise be to You. You are true, Your promise is true, the Hellfire is true, Your Word is true, Paradise is true, Your Prophets are true, the Prophet

Muḥammad (peace be upon him) is true and the Last Hour is true.

(Al-Bukhārī, *Bāb al-Tahajjud bi al-Layl*)

In deference to this divine name, we must shun all that is false and untrue.

53

THE EXCELLENT GUARDIAN

To take Allah as the only Guardian is part of our belief in Allah, as is clear from this Qur'ānic assertion: "*(O Prophet), tell them: 'He is Merciful and it is in Him that we believe and it is in Him we put all our trust.'*" (al-Mulk 67: 29) The Messengers in the Qur'ān are depicted reposing their trust in Allah and urging believers to do the same. *Tawakkul* (trust in Allah) is a highly desirable and rewarding trait which all of us should try to develop. For it reinforces our belief in the One True God. A sincere believer lives by this conviction that Allah is his best guardian. This is exemplified by the Prophet's Companions' conduct, as reported in the Qur'ān: "*When people said to them, 'Behold, a host has gathered around you and you should fear them,' it only increased their faith, and they answered: 'Allah is sufficient for us, and what an excellent Guardian He is!'*" (Āl 'Imrān 3: 173)

The Prophet (peace be upon him) referred in particular to this divine name is his supplication:

اللَّهُمَّ لَكَ أَسْلَمْتُ، وَبِكَ آمَنْتُ، وَعَلَيْكَ تَوَكَّلْتُ، وَإِلَيْكَ أَنَبْتُ، وَبِكَ خَاصَمْتُ

(البخاري، باب التهجد، ص ١١٢٠)

O Lord! I have surrendered myself to You, believed in You, reposed trust in You, turned to You and quarrelled for You.

(Al-Bukhārī, *al-Tahajjud*)

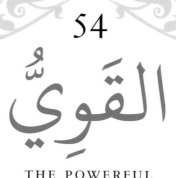

54

الْقَوِيُّ

THE POWERFUL

ALLAH is the source of all power and infuses power into everyone and everything. He strengthens our faith, our spirit and our body. The well-known Islamic liturgical formula: "*lā ḥawla wa lā quwwata illā billāh Al-ʿAlī Al-ʿAẓīm*" (There is no power or might other than that of the All-Great, Most Elevated Allah), presses home Allah's absolute power. For all help and support we should, therefore, turn to the All Powerful Allah. The following supplication is centred on the same belief:

اللَّهُمَّ إِنِّي ضَعِيفٌ فَقَوِّ بِرِضَاكَ ضُعْفِي وَخُذْ لِي الْخَيْرَ بِنَاصِيَتِي وَاجْعَلِ الْإِسْلَامَ مُنْتَهَى رِضَائِي اللَّهُمَّ إِنِّي ضَعِيفٌ فَقَوِّنِي وَإِنِّي ذَلِيلٌ فَأَعِزَّنِي وَإِنِّي فَقِيرٌ فَارْزُقْنِي

(أبو داود، الصّلاة، ص ١٥٢٢)

Right margin: *From Sūrah* al-Anfāl 8: 52

O Allah! I am weak, so strengthen my weakness in Your good pleasure. Take my forelocks to that which is good, and make Islam my ultimate good pleasure. O Allah! I am weak, so strengthen me. I am lowly, so elevate me. I am poor, so enrich me.

[Abū Dāwūd, *al-Ṣalāt*]

55

THE STRONG

BEING Self Subsistent, Allah is strong and does not experience tiredness. His strength is evident from the perfect, constant functioning of this vast universe and enforcement of His natural laws. His name *Al-Matīn* (the Strong) underscores His incessant strength, constantly at work without ever getting weary. The same truth features in the Qur'ānic *Āyat Al-Kursī* (the verse regarding Allah's dominion): "*His dominion overspreads the heavens and the earth and their upholding does not weary Him.*" (al-Baqarah 2: 255)

For attaining strength we should draw upon Him. Moreover, whenever enjoying authority we should be always humble towards Allah, Who alone is All Strong.

al-Dhāriyāt 51: 58

From Sūrah

56

THE GUARDIAN

From Sūrah al-Baqarah 2: 257

THE Qur'ān asks: "(*Are the unbelievers so foolish that*) *they have chosen others rather than Allah as their guardian? Yet it is Allah Who is the Protector and the Guardian, and Who resurrects the dead and Who has power over everything.*" (al-Shūrā 42: 9) We are given the comforting assurance: "*Allah is the Guardian of those who believe.*" (Āl ʿImrān 3: 68)

As a result, we must surrender ourselves wholly to Him and have conviction about His love for us, regularly reciting this supplication:

يَا وَلِيَّ الْإِسْلَامِ وَأَهْلِهِ ثَبِّتْنِيْ حَتَّى أَلْقَاكَ

(أبو داود، إمارة، ١٤٧)

O the Guardian of Islam and its community! Grant me peace and security until I meet You.

(Abū Dāwūd, *Imārah*)

66

57

THE MOST PRAISEWORTHY

THE significance of this divine name is evident from the first word of the opening Sūrah of the Qur'ān which commences thus: "*Praise be to Allah, the Lord of the worlds:*" (al-Fātiḥah 1: 1). Likewise, the following Qur'ānic passage explains why Allah deserves all praise: "*All praise be to Allah, the Lord of the heavens and the earth, the Lord of the worlds. His is the glory in the heavens and the earth. He is the Most Mighty, Most Wise.*" (al-Jāthiyah 45: 36–37) The Qur'ān instructs us: "*He is Allah. There is no god but He. His is the praise in this world and in the Hereafter. His is the command and to Him will all of you be returned.*" (al-Qaṣaṣ 28: 70)

References to *Ḥamd* (praise) to Allah and *Al-Ḥamīd* (Allah being the Most Praiseworthy) feature in the ṣal-awāt (invocation of blessing) which is recited in Prayers and in the Ḥajj invocation. The Prophet's following *tahajjud* supplication too, is permeated with His praise:

اَللّٰهُمَّ لَكَ الْحَمْدُ أَنْتَ قَيِّمُ السَّمٰوَاتِ وَالأَرْضِ وَمَنْ فِيهِنَّ وَلَكَ الْحَمْدُ أَنْتَ مَلِكُ السَّمٰوَاتِ وَالأَرْضِ وَمَنْ فِيهِنَّ وَلَكَ الْحَمْدُ أَنْتَ نُورُ السَّمٰوَاتِ وَالأَرْضِ وَمَنْ فِيهِنَّ وَلَكَ الْحَمْدُ أَنْتَ الْحَقُّ وَوَعْدُكَ حَقٌّ

(البخاري، التهجد، ص ١١٢٠)

O Lord! All praise is for You. You are the Self Subsisting One in the heavens and on the earth and of all those whose are in these. All praise is for You. You are the King of the heavens and the earth and of all those who are in these. All praise is for You. You are the light of the heavens and the earth and of all those who are in these. All praise is for You. You are true and Your promise is true.

(Al-Bukhārī, *al-Tahajjud*)

58

اَلْمُحْصِي

THE ONE WHO KEEPS RECORD

NOT only is Allah All-Knowing and All-Seeing, He gets everything recorded. The Qur'ān remarks: "*A chastisement shall come upon people on the Day when Allah will raise them all to a new life and will inform them of their deeds. Allah has recorded it all while they have forgotten it. Allah is a witness to everything.*" (al-Mujādalah 58: 6) Likewise, we are told about our record of deeds which will be presented before Allah on the Day of Judgment. On going through it man will exclaim: "*Woe to us! What a record is this! It leaves nothing, big or small but encompasses it.*" (al-Kahf 18: 49) We should, therefore, take special care about our actions in order to avoid embarrassment and loss in the Afterlife.

59

THE ONE WHO COMMENCES

ALLAH's greatness consists in His having created everything without anything in its pre-existent form or model: "*He excels in the creation of all that He created. He originated the creation of man from clay.*" (al-Sajdah 32: 7) Nothing exists on its own; it is only He Who brings everything into being. We should bow in adoration to our Supreme and Unique Creator.

60

THE ONE WHO RESTORES

ALLAH announces: *"He it is Who creates, for the first time and He it is Who will create again."* (al-Burūj 85: 13) This underscores His perfect knowledge and power. For the Makkan unbelievers at the time of the Prophet and for atheists today, His raising the dead to life appears incredible! Yet, as He created everything in the first place, it is of course, easy for Him to repeat the same. We should have conviction in the Afterlife as part of our sincere belief in Allah.

From Sūrah Yūnus 10: 4

61

THE ONE WHO GIVES LIFE

IT is stressed throughout the Qur'ān that Allah causes life and death. Reference here is to life in a very broad sense. At places, the Qur'ān draws our attention to the common spectacle evident to all of us: how He revives dead land which yields growth in no time. This should persuade us of His creative wonders, especially of giving life. By the same token, He will raise the dead on the Day of Judgement for His reckoning. We should earnestly pray to Allah for reviving our faith, heart and spirit.

62

THE ONE WHO CAUSES DEATH

As the master of life and death, Allah tells us: "*How can you deny Allah, Who bestowed life upon you when you were lifeless. Then He will cause you to die and will again bring you back to life so that you may be returned to Him.*" (al-Baqarah 2: 28) Reference is to man's pre-life state and his resurrection after death.

In recognition of the same truth, the Prophet (peace be upon him) taught us the following supplication which should be recited when we get up:

اَلْحَمْدُ لله الَّذِيْ أَحْيَانَا بَعْدَ مَا أَمَاتَنَا

(الترمذي، كتاب الدعوات، ص ٧٧٥)

All praise be to Allah Who brought us back to life after causing our death.

(Al-Tirmidhī, *Kitāb al-Da'awāt*)

From Sūrah al-Baqarah 2:28

⟨ 73 ⟩

63

THE EVER LIVING

ALL life in the universe is owing to Allah. For it is He alone Who grants and sustains life. This name figures prominently in *Āyat Al-Kursī* (al-Baqarah 2: 255) which stresses Allah's absolute power. We are directed to invoke Him, using this name: "*He is the Ever Living. There is no god but He. So call upon Him, making your devotion exclusive to Him*". (al-Mu'min 40: 65)

64

الْقَيُّومُ

THE SELF-SUBSISTING

THIS divine name emphasizes Allah's uniqueness and supremacy and underlines His eternal being. On the Day of Judgement "*all faces shall be humbled before the Ever-Living, Self-Subsisting Lord*". (Ṭā Hā 20: 111) While all living beings are mortal, He being the Self-Subsisting has always been and will be there as the Ever-Living.

Whenever faced with a crisis, the Prophet (peace be upon him) used to address Allah with this name, as is evident from the following Ḥadīth reports:

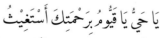

يَا حَيُّ يَا قَيُّومُ بِرَحْمَتِكَ أَسْتَغِيثُ

(أحمد مسند أحمد ٥/ ٤٢ ابن حبان، الموارد، ٢٣٧٠)

O the Ever-Living One, the Self-Subsisting One! I invoke Your mercy.

(Aḥmad/Ibn Hibbān, *Al-Mawārid*)

He directed his daughter, Fāṭimah, to recite this supplication:

يَا حَيُّ يَا قَيُّومُ بِرَحْمَتِكَ أَسْتَغِيثُ فَلَا تَكِلْنِيْ إِلَى نَفْسِيْ طَرْفَةَ عَيْنٍ
(الترمذي، كتاب الدعوات، ص ٩٢)

O the Ever-Living One, the Self-Subsisting One, I invoke Your mercy. Do not leave me to myself even for the twinkling of the eye.

(Al-Tirmidhī, *Kitāb Al-Daʿawāt*)

65

الْقَرِيبُ

THE NEAR

ALLAH tells the Prophet (peace be upon him) in the Qur'ān: "(*O Muḥammaḍ*), *when My servants ask you about Me, tell them I am quite near; I hear and answer the call of the caller whenever he calls Me.*" (al-Baqarah 2: 186) Allah's closeness is pressed home in the following Ḥadīth: "Abū Mūsā al-Ashʿarī reports that as some Companions, on the way to the Khyber battle, recited aloud, *Allāhu Akbar* (Allah is Great), the Prophet told them: '*We are comforted by the Qur'ānic assertion that Allah's mercy is close to those who do good.*'" (al-Aʿrāf 7: 56) Since He is All-Hearing, All-Seeing and Ever Responsive, His nearness to humankind is plausible.

Hūd 11: 61

From Sūrah

❧ 77 ❧

66

THE GLORIOUS

ALLAH's glory is self-evident in that He is Matchless and Supreme. The following Prophetic supplication instructs us how to celebrate His glory:

Kitāb al-Duʿāʾ: 3,861

سُبْحَانَ الَّذِيْ تَعَطَّفَ بِالْعِزَّةِ وَ سُبْحَانَ الَّذِيْ لَبِسَ الْمَجْدِ وَتَكَرَّمَ بِهِ وَسُبْحَانَ ذِي الْمَجْدِ وَالْكَرَمِ سُبْحَانَ ذِي الْجَلَالِ وَالْإِكْرَامِ

(الطبراني، عن ابن عباس، ٤٢٩)

Glory be to Allah Who embodies all honour. Glory be to Allah Who is full of majesty and exaltation. Glory be to Allah Who is Most Glorious, Noblest. Glory be to Allah, full of majesty and splendour.

(Al-Ṭabarānī, on the authority of Ibn ʿAbbās)

From Ibn Mājah

67

THE ONE GOD

THE belief in the One True God is central to the Islamic belief system. This conviction keeps us away from associating anyone or, anything, with Him. Allah's Oneness is emphasized throughout the Qur'ān in a variety of ways. This true belief in Allah's unicity will help us attain deliverance on the Day of Judgement.

Several Aḥādīth direct us to reinvigorate our faith by reciting the supplications taught by the Prophet (peace be upon him).

لَاإِلَهَ إِلَّا اللهُ وَحْدَهُ لَا شَرِيْكَ لَهُ، لَهُ الْمُلْكُ وَلَهُ الْحَمْدُ وَهُوَ عَلَى كُلِّ شَيْءٍ قَدِيْرٌ، اَللَّهُمَّ مَا أَصْبَحَ بِيْ مِنْ نِعْمَةٍ أَوْ بِأَحَدٍ مِنْ خَلْقِكَ فَمِنْكَ وَحْدَكَ لَا شَرِيْكَ لَكَ فَلَكَ الْحَمْدُ وَلَكَ الشُّكْرُ

(أبو داود، الادب ٥٠٧٣)

There is no god besides Allah. He does not have any partner. For Him is the kingdom and for Him is all

praise. He has power over everything. O Allah, any blessing that I or anyone else of Your creation possess this morning is from You alone, You have no partner. All praise and all thanks are due to You.

(Abū Dāwūd, *Al-Adab*)

68

THE ONE

AL-AḤAD represents the uniqueness of the One True God, while *Al-Wāḥid* refers to His indivisible wholeness and oneness. *Aḥad* is used for Allah in the sense that He is One and Unique in every respect, Who has no connection whatsoever with plurality. That is why *Aḥad* is used in Arabic exclusively for Allah. Accordingly, in Sūrah *Al-Ikhlāṣ* the divine name *Al-Aḥad* is used in the above sense: "*Say, He is Allah, the One and Unique* […] *and none is comparable to Him.*" (al-Ikhlāṣ 112: 1 and 4)

In view of the importance of this divine attribute, our words and deeds should reflect only monotheism, without even an iota of polytheism. Our sincere commitment to the One True God may help us attain His pleasure.

69

الصَّمَدُ

THE UNIQUE

WE learn from Sūrah *al-Ikhlāṣ* that Allah is unique in the sense that He is not in need of anyone, while everyone is in need of Him. His uniqueness is self-evident in terms of birth, life and death. He has eternally existed before He brought anyone or thing into being or caused it to die. Nor is there anyone comparable to Him in the remotest degree.

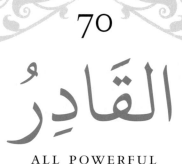

70

الْقَادِرُ

ALL POWERFUL

DERIVED from the Qur'ānic verse: "*Allah has the power to what He wills*" (al-Mursalāt 77: 23), this divine name should make us realize that the All-Powerful has created and set everything according to His pre-ordained scheme (*taqdīr*). All that we get, ranging from food and money to our life span, has already been determined by Him out of His infinite wisdom. We should, nonetheless, pray to Him for what we want. We should also strengthen our conviction that no one other than Allah can take away what He has decreed for us.

From Sūrah al-Mursalāt 77: 23

71

الْمُقْتَدِرُ

THE MIGHTY IN POWER

IT is the intensive form of *Al-Qadīr*. Accordingly, the following Qur'ānic verses employing this expression draw our attention to His might in seizing everyone and His might as the King: "*Thereupon We seized them with the seizing of the Most Mighty, the Most Powerful*" (al-Qamar 54: 42) and "*where they will be honourably seated in the presence of a King, Mighty in Power*". (al-Qamar 54: 55) In view of His exalted status we are obliged to worship and obey Him.

72

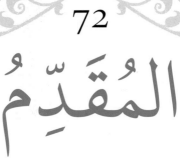

THE WARNER

THE Qur'ān describes clearly how Allah deals with man: "*I have warned you. My Word does not change. Nor do I inflict the least wrong upon My servants.*" (Qāf 50: 28–29)

Through His books and Messengers sent by Him down the ages, in almost all parts of the world, Allah has warned people against the dire consequences of not accepting faith. His message has remained consistently the same: Worship and serve the One True God.

May Allah enable all of us to pay attention to His warnings.

73

THE ONE WHO DEFERS

From Sunan Al-Dārimī I: ١,٤٨٦

Out of His infinite wisdom Allah most often defers punishing the guilty. Other instances in point are the after effects of things, and reward and punishment for our actions. His deferring of certain things is part of His broader scheme. The absence of immediate recompense for our misdeeds should not be misinterpreted in the sense that we can get away. He defers His decision only up to a point of time. In our case, death is the terminus after which we cannot improve our record of deeds. This should make us all the more careful about His Judgement which is imminent, though we may not be instantly rewarded or punished.

أَنْتَ ٱلْمُقَدِّمُ وَأَنْتَ ٱلْمُؤَخِّرُ لَا إِلَهَ إِلَّا أَنْتَ وَلَا حَوْلَ وَلَا قُوَّةَ إِلَّا بِكَ

(الدارمي، باب الدعاء، ج-١، ١٤٨٦)

O Allah! You are the First and the Last. There is no
god besides You. There is no power or authority except Yours.

(Al-Dārimī, *Bāb al-Du'ā'*)

74

الأَوَّلُ

THE FIRST

ALLAH precedes everyone and everything. Others exist only in relation to Him being the First One. As everyone has to return to Him, He stands out as the First and Foremost One.

The Prophet (peace be upon him) taught this supplication to his daughter, Fāṭimah, which makes a special mention of Him as the first:

اَللّٰهُمَّ رَبَّ السَّمٰوَاتِ السَّبْعِ وَرَبَّ الْعَرْشِ الْعَظِيمِ رَبَّنَا وَرَبَّ كُلِّ شَيْءٍ مُنْزِلَ التَّوْرَاةِ وَالْإِنْجِيلِ وَالْقُرْآنِ فَالِقَ الْحَبِّ وَالنَّوىٰ أَعُوذُ بِكَ مِنْ شَرِّ كُلِّ شَيْءٍ أَنْتَ آخِذٌ بِنَاصِيَتِهِ أَنْتَ الْأَوَّلُ فَلَيْسَ قَبْلَكَ شَيْءٌ

(الترمذي، كتاب الدعوات، ص ٧٩٠)

O Lord of the seven heavens and of the mighty throne! You are our Lord and of our everything. You

revealed the Torah, the Gospel and the Qur'ān. You split the grain and kernel of fruit, I seek refuge in You from the evil of any who possesses evil. It is You Who will restrain him by the forelock. You are the First one; there is nothing before You.

(Al-Tirmidhī, *Kitāb al-Da'awāt*)

75

الآخِرُ

THE LAST

ALLAH is the Last One, in that everyone has to return to Him. He is the Last in the sense of being the Eternal and the Ever Lasting. Reference to this excellent name of Allah occurs in the following supplication taught by the Prophet (peace be upon him) to his daughter, Fāṭimah:

اَللَّهُمَّ رَبَّ ٱلسَّمَـٰوَاتِ السَّبْعِ وَ رَبَّ الْعَرْشِ الْعَظِيْمِ رَبَّنَا وَرَبَّ كُلِّ شَيْءٍ مُنْزِلَ التَّوْرَاةِ وَالْإِنْجِيْلِ وَ الْقُرْآنِ فَالِقَ الْحَبِّ وَ النَّوىٰ أَعُوْذُبِكَ مِنْ شَرِّ كُلِّ شَيْءٍ أَنْتَ آخِذٌ بِنَاصِيَتِه أَنْتَ الْأَوَّلُ فَلَيْسَ قَبْلَكَ شَيْءٌ وَ أَنْتَ الْآخِرُ فَلَيْسَ بَعْدَكَ شَيْءٌ

(الترمذي، كتاب الدعوات، ص ٧٩٠)

O Lord of the seven heavens and of the mighty throne! You are our Lord and of our everything. You revealed the Torah, the Gospel and the Qur'ān. You

al-Ḥadīd 57: 3

From Sūrah

❧ 90 ❧

split the grain and kernel of fruit, I seek refuge in You from the evil of any who possesses evil. It is You Who will restrain him by the forelock. You are the First one; there is nothing before You. You are the Last one; there is nothing after You.

(Al-Tirmidhī, *Kitāb al-Daʿawāt*)

76

الظَّاهِرُ

THE MANIFEST

ALLAH'S creative wonders and truth are manifest everywhere, open to everyone. All that exists serves as a sign and manifestation of His being, His power and His knowledge. Moreover, He lavishes manifest bounties upon us. The Qur'ān points to the same: "*Have you not seen that Allah has subjected to your service all that is in the heavens and on the earth and has abundantly bestowed upon you His bounties, both visible and invisible?*" (Luqmān 31: 20)

77

الْبَاطِنُ

THE HIDDEN

THE meaning of this divine name is elucidated by
this Qur'ānic verse: "*No visual perception can encompass
Him, even though He encompasses all visual perception.*"
(al-Anʿām 6: 103) He bestows upon us inner bounties
which illuminate our souls.

78

THE MOST HIGH

THE Qur'ān designates Allah as: "*the Supreme One, the Most High*". (al-Raʿd 13: 9) Since He excels over everyone, He must be taken as the Most High. At places, the Qur'ān says that He is far above the unbelievers' associating others as partners with Him, or their ascribing baseless things to Him or their saying things about Him which do not befit Him. He, being the Most High, is indeed far above their fabrications.

As His servants we should be in awe of the Most High and serve Him with utmost humility.

79

THE MOST BENIGN

FOR His numerous favours to us and His provision of Paradise for us, Allah must be taken as the Most Benign. Other manifestations of the same are: His sending down of the Qur'ān and the Prophet Muḥammad (peace be upon him). Through our word and deed we should thank Him for His tremendous kindness to us.

From Sūrah al-Ṭūr 52:28

80

التَّوَّابُ

THE MUCH RELENTING

From Sūrah al-Baqarah 2: 37

OUT of His boundless mercy Allah forgives us. The Qur'ān informs: "*Allah it is Who accepts repentance from His servants and forgives sins and knows all what you do.*" (al-Shūrā 42: 25) Nonetheless, our repentance should be genuine and sincere, marked by our conviction not to repeat that wrong.

In response to Allah's excellent promise of relenting towards us, we should immediately utilize this opportunity of seeking His repentance. It will contribute to our moral and spiritual elevation and prepare ourselves better for the Next Life.

81

المُنْتَقِمُ

THE ONE WHO INFLICTS RETRIBUTION

BEING Just and All Powerful, Allah exacts retribution, as He tells: *"We sent Messengers before you [O Prophet Muḥammad], to their respective nations, and they brought clear signs to them. Then We took vengeance upon those who acted wickedly. It was incumbent upon Us to come to the aid of the believers."* (al-Rūm 30: 47) We should seek always Allah's protection against His retribution.

From Sūrah al-Aʿrāf 7: 136

82

اَلْعَفُوُّ

THE ALL RELENTING

SINCE Allah is Most Forgiving, He teaches us to forgive others. (al-Aʿrāf 7: 199) Islam stands for compassion, mutual love and sincere cooperation.

ʿĀʾishah reports that the Prophet (peace be upon him) had taught her this supplication to be recited on the last ten blessed nights of Ramadan:

اَللَّهُمَّ إِنَّكَ عَفُوٌّ كَرِيمٌ تُحِبُّ الْعَفْوَ فَاعْفُ عَنِّي

(الترمذي، كتاب الدعوات، ص ٧٩٨)

O Lord! You are All Relenting, the Noblest. You love forgiving. So forgive me.

(Al-Tirmidhī, *Kitāb al-Daʿawāt*)

83

الرَّؤُوفُ

THE ONE FULL OF GENTLENESS

ALLAH's gentleness towards His creatures is universal, cutting across all boundaries. He is gentle to even those who openly rebel against Him. His bounties, sustenance and concern for their success in the Next Life are reflective of His abundant gentleness. We should draw upon His gentleness and as thanksgiving we should adhere to the way of life prescribed by Him.

From Sūrah al-Baqarah 2: 143

84

مَالِكُ
المُلْكِ

LORD OF ALL DOMINION

Āl ʿImrān 3: 26

From Sūrah

NOT only is Allah the King, He is truly the King of all Kings. For all dominion belongs solely to Him. And His writ prevails everywhere.

This divine appellation establishes His omnipotence and supremacy. All pale into insignificance in comparison to Him. He is simply matchless, unrivalled in His strength and power.

We should surrender wholly to the Lord of all dominion and seek His mercy.

85

ذُو الْجَلَالِ وَالْإِكْرَامِ

FULL OF MAJESTY AND SPLENDOUR

THE Qur'ān states this truth for our reflection: "*All that is on earth will perish, only the Being of your Lord, full of majesty and splendour will endure.*" (al-Raḥmān 55: 27) We are accordingly asked to glorify Him. We should not suffer from any delusion of greatness, no matter how many favours are bestowed upon us. For true power, greatness and glory belong only to Allah.

86

المُقْسِطُ

THE ONE WHO ACTS JUSTLY

From Al-Tirmidhī   Kitāb Al-Daʿawāt: 3,507

THROUGHOUT the Qur'ān we are exhorted to act justly. It is plainly stated that Allah does not love the unjust. Rather, He will punish them badly. He sent down His Scriptures and Messengers for establishing and promoting justice. It is binding upon us to profess and enjoin justice.

87

THE ONE WHO GATHERS

Not only has Allah provided minerals, plants, animals and human beings on the planet earth, He will gather all on the Day of Judgement: "*Our Lord! One Day You will gather all mankind together, the Day about which there is no doubt. Surely Allah never goes against His promise.*" (Āl 'Imrān 3: 9)

We should always be ready for death and our accountability to Allah on the Day of Judgement.

From Sūrah Āl 'Imrān 3: 9

88

THE ALL SUFFICIENT

From Sūrah al-Baqarah 2: 263

THE Qur'ān informs us that: *"Allah does not stand in need of anyone in the whole universe."* (Āl 'Imrān 3: 97) He keeps lavishing His bounties on everyone. Likewise, He answers the prayers of those in need of Him. On reflection it is realized that all of us, no matter how well placed some of us might be, badly need others for meeting our basic needs. However, Allah being Unique and All-Powerful is such that He does not need anyone. Even, worshipping and praising Him, which is emphasized much in Islam, is not at all needed by Him. He has prescribed it only as a test for us in order to ascertain as to who obeys Him unseen.

89

المُغْنِي

THE ONE WHO ENRICHES

ALLAH promised Muslims in the Qur'ān: "*If they (believers) are poor, Allah will enrich them out of His bounty.*" (al-Nūr 24: 32) This promise came true, as Muslims gained control over major parts of the world in a short space of time. His enriching is not related only to material resources; it covers also spiritual and emotional reinforcement. We should pray to Allah for lavishing His grace upon us which will enrich us both materially and spiritually.

From Sūrah *al-Nūr 24: 33*

90

THE ONE WHO GIVES

ALLAH promises pious believers: "*As for those who are blessed, they shall abide in Paradise as long as the heavens and the earth last, unless your Lord should will otherwise. They shall enjoy an unending gift.*" (Hūd 11: 108) Allah gives us in abundance a variety of things in this life and will provide even more in Paradise.

We should thank and serve our Gracious Lord Who keeps bestowing His bounties on us.

91

THE ONE WHO FORBIDS

In His capacity as the Lord Who Knows best what is in our interest, He has forbidden certain food items and sins.

The Prophet (peace be upon him) used to offer this supplication after every Prayer:

اَللَّهُمَّ لَا مَانِعَ لِمَا أَعْطَيْتَ وَلَا مُعْطِيَ لِمَا مَنَعْتَ وَلَا يَنْفَعُ ذَا الْجَدِّ مِنْكَ الْجَدُّ

(البخاري، في صفة الصّلاة، ج-٧، ص ٢٣٧)

O Lord! There is no one to stop from what You give and there is no one to give what You stop. Nor can anyone besides You give any benefit.

(Al-Bukhārī, *Fī Ṣifat al-Ṣalāt*)

Kitāb al-Duʿāʾ: 3,861

From Ibn Mājāh

92

النَّافِعُ

THE BENEFICENT

From Sūrah   al-Fatḥ 48: 11

THE Qur'ān is crystal clear on the point that it is Allah alone Who benefits or harms man: "*Who can be of any avail to you against Allah if He should intend to cause you any harm or confer upon you any benefit.*" (al-Fatḥ 48: 11) Even the Prophet (peace be upon him), despite his elevated position, has "*no power to benefit or harm*" himself or others. (al-Aʿrāf 7: 188) In view of His omnipotence Allah alone is in a position to shower upon us the bounties which He wills.

This should deter us from approaching anyone other than Him for seeking favours. We should implore only Him for all that we need.

93

الـنُّورُ

THE LIGHT

THE Qur'ān provides this admirable description of Allah Whose Being is otherwise hard to comprehend: "*Allah is the light of the heavens and the earth. His light (in the universe) may be likened to a niche wherein is a lamp, and the lamp is in the crystal which shines in star-like brilliance. It is lit from (the oil) of a blessed olive tree that is neither eastern nor western. Its oil well-nigh glows forth (of itself) though no fire touched it. Light upon light.*" (al-Nūr 24: 35) The Qur'ān designates faith, guidance and truth as light. In view of the association of light with Allah, the Prophet's following supplication contains a refrain like reference to light:

اَللّهُمَّ اجْعَلْ فِي قَلْبِي نُوراً وَاجْعَلْ فِي لِسَانِي نُوراً وَاجْعَلْ فِي سَمْعِي نُوراً وَاجْعَلْ فِي بَصَرِيْ نُوراً وَاجْعَلْ خَلْفِي نُوراً وَأَمَامِي نُوراً وَاجْعَلْ

From Sūrah   al-Nūr 24: 35

مِنْ فَوْقِي نُوراً وَمِنْ تَحْتِيْ نُوراً اَللَّهُمَّ وَأَعْظِمْ لِيْ نُوراً لَا يَذِلُّ مَنْ
وَالَيْتُ وَلَا يَعِزُّ مَنْ عَادَيْتُ

(أبو داود، كتاب الصّلاة، ص ٢٣٣)

O Allah! Place light in my heart, light in my tongue, light in my hearing, light in my sight, light behind me, light in front of me, light above me and light below me. O Allah! magnify my light. Indeed he whom You have taken under Your custody shall not be humiliated. Nor will he against whom You have declared enmity gain any might.

(Abū Dāwūd, *Kitāb Al-Ṣalāt*)

94

الهَادِي

THE GUIDE

ALLAH's guidance for us is at various levels:

(i) "*He gives everything its form and then guides it.*" (Ṭā Hā 20: 50) What is meant is that after creating each being on a certain pattern Allah teaches each how they should function and fulfil the purpose of their creation. As a result, fish swim and birds fly.

(ii) He sends down Messengers "*who guide people by His command*". (al-Sajdah 32: 24)

(iii) "*Allah's guidance to His way is for those who strive in His cause.*" (al-ʿAnkabūt 29: 69) This is a particularly great assurance for us. Provided we sincerely serve His cause, He will constantly open new avenues for guidance. At each step He will instruct us about the ways through which we can achieve His good pleasure.

From Sūrah al-Fātiḥah 1: 5

Seeking His guidance is thus incumbent on us. While reciting Sūrah *al-Fātiḥah* in each *rakʿah* of our Prayer we implore Him: "*Guide us to the straight way, the way of those whom You have favoured, who did not incur Your wrath and who are not astray.*" (al-Fātiḥah 1: 5–7)

95

الْبَدِيعُ

THE ORIGINATOR

———— ◆ ————

ALLAH is not only the Creator but, also, the Orig-
inator of all that exists. For He brought everything
into being out of nothing. This calls for our greater
appreciation of His creative wonders visible in and
around ourselves.

From Sūrah al-Baqarah 2: 117

96

الْبَاقِي

THE ONE WHO REMAINS

————— ·◆· —————

WHILE all are subject to death, Allah alone will remain forever. The Qur'ān presents this truth: "*All that is on earth will perish, only the being of Your Lord, full of majesty and splendour, will endure.*" (al-Raḥmān 55: 26–27) One manifestation of His uniqueness is that He has always existed and will continue so for ever.

This should alert us to our brief life and our ultimate return to Him. He will decide our fate on the basis of our actions.

From Sūrah Ṭā Hā 20:73

97

THE OWNER

ALLAH is the true Owner of all that exists. We draw temporarily on what we possess. We, however, leave behind everything when we die. It is only Allah Who ultimately owns everything.

Given this, we should regard ourselves only as trustees of our belongings and give out of these what is due to the poor and the needy. Allah, being the real Master and Owner, will call us to account regarding our belongings.

From Sūrah al-Ḥijr 15:23

98

الرَّشِيدُ

THE GUIDE

ALLAH guides believers, as is stated in the Qur'ān: "*Allah has endeared faith to you and has embellished it in your hearts, and has made unbelief and evil doing and disobedience abhorrent to you. Such are those who are rightly guided.*" (al-Ḥujurāt 49: 7)

The above passage is like a mirror in which we should examine our conduct and assess how much we follow the above guidance.

Kitāb al-Daʿawāt 3, 507

From Al-Tirmidhī

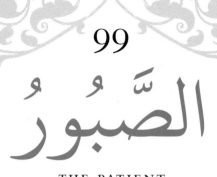

99

الصَّبُورُ

THE PATIENT

———•◦•———

THIS is amply borne out by both the Qurʾān and Ḥadīth that Allah graciously puts up with numerous despicable and outrageous forms of polytheism. As He is All-Powerful, He can obliterate the guilty in no time. Yet, He keeps granting them respite so that they may mend their ways and return to the straight way in their own interest.

Allah is the source of granting patience to man. The Qurʾān directs Muslims: "*Believers, be steadfast and vie in steadfastness, stand firm in your faith, and hold Allah in fear that you may attain true success*". (Āl ʿImrān 3: 200)

INDEX

Excellent Names and Attributes of Allah

21	Al-Wahhāb	الوَهَّابُ
22	Al-Razzāq	الرَّزَّاقُ
23	Al-Fattāḥ	الفَتَّاحُ
24	Al-ʿAlīm	العَلِيمُ
25	Al-Qābiḍ	القَابِضُ
26	Al-Bāsiṭ	البَاسِطُ
27	Al-Khāfiḍ	الـخَافِضُ
28	Al-Rāfiʿ	الرَّافِعُ
29	Al-Muʿizz	الـمُعِزُّ
31	Al-Mudhill	الـمُذِلُّ
32	Al-Samīʿ	السَّمِيعُ
33	Al-Baṣīr	البَصِيرُ
34	Al-Ḥakam	الـحَكَمُ
35	Al-ʿĀlim	العَالِمُ
36	Al-Laṭīf	اللَّطِيفُ
37	Al-Khabīr	الـخَبِيرُ
38	Al-Ḥalīm	الـحَلِيمُ
39	Al-ʿAẓīm	العَظِيمُ
40	Al-Ghafūr	الغَفُورُ
41	Al-Shakūr	الشَّكُورُ
42	Al-Aʿlā	الأَعْلَىٰ
43	Al-Kabīr	الكَبِيرُ

44	Al-Ḥafīẓ	الـحَفِيظُ
45	Al-Muqīt	الـمُقِيتُ
46	Al-Ḥasīb	الـحَسِيبُ
47	Al-Jalīl	الـجَلِيلُ
48	Al-Karīm	الكَرِيمُ
49	Al-Raqīb	الرَّقِيبُ
50	Al-Mujīb	الـمُجِيبُ
51	Al-Wāsi'	الوَاسِعُ
52	Al-Ḥakīm	الـحَكِيمُ
53	Al-Wadūd	الوَدُودُ
55	Al-Majīd	الـمَجِيدُ
56	Al-Bā'ith	البَاعِثُ
57	Al-Shahīd	الشَّهِيدُ
59	Al-Ḥaqq	الـحَقُّ
61	Al-Wakīl	الوَكِيلُ
63	Al-Qawwī	القَوِيُّ
65	Al-Matīn	الـمَتِينُ
66	Al-Walī	الوَلِيُّ
67	Al-Ḥamīd	الـحَمِيدُ
69	Al-Muḥṣī	الـمُحْصِيُ
70	Al-Mubdi'	الـمُبْدِئ
71	Al-Mu'īd	الـمُعِيدُ

72	Al-Muḥyī	الـمُحْيِّ
73	Al-Mumīt	الـمُمِيتُ
74	Al-Ḥayy	الـحَيُّ
75	Al-Qayyūm	القَيُّومُ
77	Al-Qarīb	القَرِيبُ
78	Al-Mājid	الـمَاجِدُ
79	Al-Wāḥid	الوَاحِدُ
81	Al-Aḥad	الأَحَدُ
82	Al-Ṣamad	الصَّمَدُ
83	Al-Qādir	القَادِرُ
84	Al-Muqtadir	الـمُقْتَدِرُ
85	Al-Muqaddim	الـمُقَدِّمُ
86	Al-Mu'akhkhir	الـمُؤَخِّرُ
88	Al-Awwal	الأَوَّلُ
90	Al-Ākhir	الآخِرُ
92	Al-Ẓāhir	الظَّاهِرُ
93	Al-Bāṭin	البَاطِنُ
94	Al-Muta'āl	الـمُتَعَالِ
95	Al-Barr	البَرُّ
96	Al-Tawwāb	التَّوَّابُ
97	Al-Muntaqim	الـمُنْتَقِمُ
98	Al-'Afuww	العَفُوُّ

99	Al-Ra'ūf	الرَّؤُوفُ
100	Mālik Al-Mulk	مَالِكُ الـمُلكِ
101	Dhū Al-Jalāl wa Al-Ikrām	ذُو الـجَلالِ والإِكْرَامِ
102	Al-Muqsiṭ	الـمُقْسِطُ
103	Al-Jāmi'	الـجَامِعُ
104	Al-Ghanī	الغَنِيُّ
105	Al-Mughnī	الـمُغْنِيُّ
106	Al-Mu'ṭī	الـمُعْطِيُّ
107	Al-Māni'	الـمَانِعُ
108	Al-Nāfi'	النَّافِعُ
109	Al-Nūr	النُّورُ
111	Al-Hādī	الـهَادِي
113	Al-Badī'	البَدِيعُ
114	Al-Bāqī	البَاقِي
115	Al-Wārith	الوَارِثُ
116	Al-Rashīd	الرَّشِيدُ
117	Al-Ṣabūr	الصَّبُورُ

NOTES

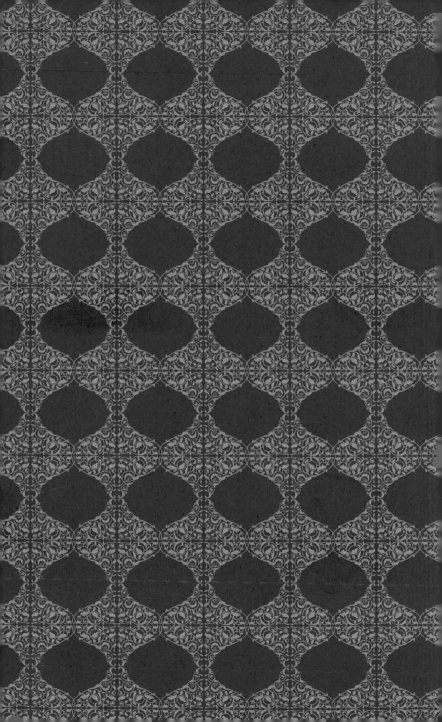